The Five Senses

Touching

Rebecca Rissman

Heinemann Library
Chicago, Illinois

www.heinemannraintree.com
Visit our website to find out
more information about
Heinemann-Raintree books.

To order:

☎ Phone 888-454-2279

💻 Visit www.heinemannraintree.com
to browse our catalog and order online.

Edited by Rebecca Rissman and Catherine Veitch
Designed by Ryan Frieson and Kimberly R. Miracle
Original illustrations © Capstone Global Library
Illustrated by Tony Wilson (pp. 11, 12, 22, 23)
Picture research by Tracy Cummins
Originated by Heinemann Library
Printed in China by South China Printing Company Ltd

14 13 12 11 10
10 9 8 7 6 5 4 3 2

Library of Congress Cataloging-in-Publication Data
Touching / Rebecca Rissman.
p. cm. -- (The five senses)
ISBN 978-1-4329-3682-2 (hc) -- ISBN 978-1-4329-3688-4 (pb)
QP451.R39 2010
 612.8'8--dc22
2009022289

Acknowledgments
The author and publishers are grateful to the following for permission
to reproduce copyright material: Alamy pp. 13 (© Jack Sullivan), 16 (©
Kader Meguedad); Corbis pp. 4 (© David P. Hall), 15 (© Andrzej Grygiel/
PAP), 20 (© Markus Altmann); Getty Images pp. 5 (MoMo Productions),
6 (Bruno Morandi), 7 (Hitoshi Nishimura), 9 (Keiji Iwai), 10 (Marc
Oeder), 14 (Livia Corona), 17 (Mark Hall), 18 (Macduff Everton), 19 (Jose
Luis Pelaez); Shutterstock pp. 8 (© Melanie DeFazio), 21 (© Karin Lau),
23 C (© Melanie DeFazio).

Cover photograph of a hand touching the surface of still mountain water
reproduced with permission of Getty Images (Philip and Karen Smith).
Back cover photograph of a girl stroking a kitten reproduced with
permission of Shutterstock (© Melanie DeFazio).

The publishers would like to thank Nancy Harris, Yael Biederman, and
Matt Siegel for their assistance in the preparation of this book.

Every effort has been made to contact copyright holders of any material
reproduced in this book. Any omissions will be rectified in subsequent
printings if notice is given to the publisher.

Contents

Senses 4

How Do You Touch? 8

What Do You Touch? 14

Using Touch 20

Naming the Parts
   You Use to Touch 22

Picture Glossary 23

Index 24

Senses

We all have five senses.

We use our senses every day.

Touching and seeing are senses.

Tasting, smelling, and hearing are also senses.

How Do You Touch?

You feel the things you touch.

skin

You feel things on your skin.

Nerves under your skin help you to feel.

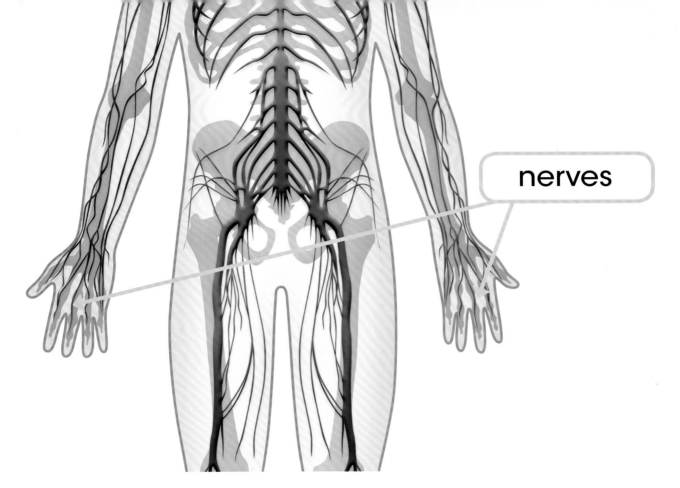

nerves

Nerves are like string.

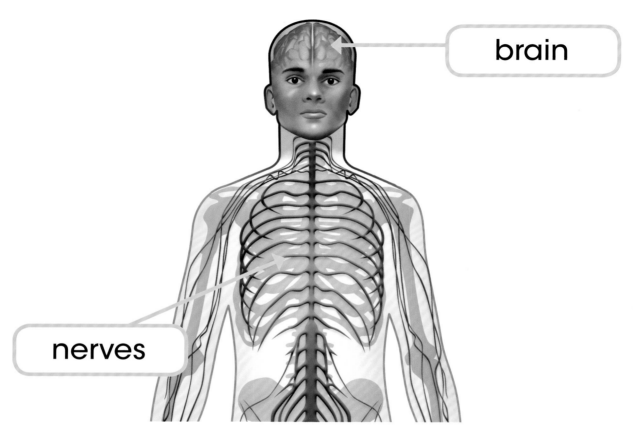

brain

nerves

Nerves tell your brain how things feel.

Your brain tells you what you are feeling.

What Do You Touch?

You can touch many different things.

Things can feel very different.

You can touch things that feel rough. A tree trunk feels rough.

You can touch things that feel smooth.
A glass window feels smooth.

You can touch things that feel hot.
Sand can feel hot.

You can touch things that feel cold.
Snow feels cold.

Some people do not see.

They feel the things around them.

Naming the Parts You Use to Touch

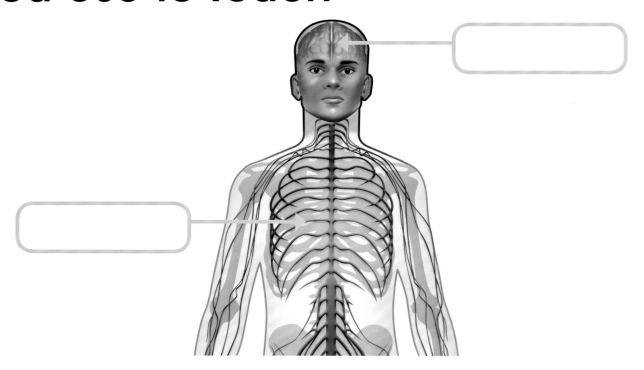

Point to where these labels should go.

brain   nerves

Answer on page 12.

Picture Glossary

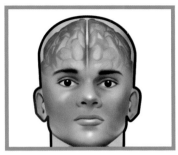

brain part of your body that helps you think, remember, feel, and move

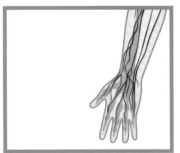

nerves body parts that carry messages about feelings between your brain and other parts of your body

sense something that helps you smell, see, touch, taste, and hear things around you

Index

brain 12, 13, 23   skin 9, 10

nerves 10, 11, 12, 23   touching 6, 8, 14, 16–17, 18–19, 20, 22

senses 4, 5, 6, 7, 23

Note to Parents and Teachers

Before reading

Explain to children that people use five senses to understand the world: seeing, hearing, tasting, touching, and smelling. Tell children that there are different body parts associated with each sense. Then ask children which body parts they think they use to touch. Tell children they use their skin to touch things. Explain that nerves that run under the skin send messages to the brain.

After reading

• Show children the diagram of the sensory system on page 22. Ask them to point to where the labels "brain" and "nerves" should go.

• Make a "feeling box" to put objects in. Ask children to put their hand in the box and feel what's inside. Can they guess what's in the box? Can they describe it?

• Ask children to work in pairs, with one child wearing a blindfold. Ask the other child in each pair to help their partner feel their way around the room. How did the child wearing the blindfold feel? Did feeling things help them to guess where they were?